THE NEVER ENDING BRAINSTORM

A Blueprint for Democracy

DEDICATION

First and foremost, this book is dedicated to the memory of Joseph Verderber. At only 25 years old, his life was cut short in February 2016, barely a month after he had stood by my side as a groomsman on my wedding day. Joey was the first person I met in college and was one of my closest friends from that moment on. He shared my ideals for positive social change, and we were working on a platform that embodies the ideals of this book in a way that allows people to interact. When he passed, that project faded and I began putting all of this down on paper. Thank you for giving me the push I needed to get these ideas organized, and for reminding me that every person has a special gift that cannot be replaced.

Secondly, I would like to dedicate this book to the memory of Sean Henry. Another great soul taken too early, just one year later in February 2017. After extensive edits and peer reviews, my writing had started slowing down and I began to get discouraged that the book wasn't coming together exactly the way I thought it should. Sean was a gentle reminder that the goal is to always have love for all people, and that putting others first is the only way to create change in the world. Thank you for the push you gave me to finish this, and for the joy that you shared with everyone.

There are hundreds of people who have continued to help me shape and reform these ideas since I started seeking answers at a young age. This is dedicated to my parents, my siblings, extended family, and all close acquaintances from around the world. To all of those that simply pointed me in the right ideological direction, or sat down and shared your ideas with mine to help sharpen both of ours, or even the few of you who read the whole thing first and provided valuable edits, I thank you.

Last, but definitely not least, I dedicate this to my perfect, beautiful, supportive, and loving bride, Chloe. Thank you for sticking with me through thick and thin. Thank you for always supporting my dreams, and for always following your own at the same time. Thank you for always being patient with me, and for the countless hours spent pouring yourself into these pages with me. Thank you for being infinitely better than I am at naming things, and particularly for naming The Never Ending Brainstorm itself! Most importantly, thank you for giving me passion and a purpose. You are my continual inspiration, and I will love you forever.

CONTENTS

Prologue   9

Part 1: The Organization of Thought   17

    Logic and The Scientific Method   19

    Applying Logic to Life   27

    Philosophy, Religion, and Science   35

    Hard Sciences versus Soft Sciences   41

Part 2: The Origins of Societal Flaws   47

    The Evolution of Political Flaws   49

    The Evolution of Economic Flaws   55

Part 3: Changes to Modern Society   61

    Education Reform   63

    Political Reform   73

    Economic Reform   85

Closing Thoughts   97

Epilogue   101

PROLOGUE

Intentional Societal Evolution

To my friends, family, and ideally, some strangers. There is nothing more important to me than the well-being of people in general, and I look forward to hearing your critique of my ideas and working together to improve society. This is the kind of thing that you might wish there was a summary for, but unfortunately, this is the summary. My life's goal has been to study our society and political system, and try to come up with solutions to our major problems. What I have found is that we systematically treat symptoms of societal problems instead of the root causes.

It's as if there were a house that had a window that kept breaking. You might replace the window, then re-enforce the glass, then re-enforce the wall, but if you never take the time to realize that the whole house is simply sitting on a shaky foundation, the window will keep breaking. I believe that the solutions to our problems are not only right in front of us, but extremely simple and easy to implement.

> *We systematically treat symptoms of societal problems instead of the root causes.*

9

Regardless of what your personal beliefs are, if it is your goal to improve the quality of your own life and the lives of the people around you, then we are on the same page. My one request is that you do not turn away from this just because you find certain points that you disagree with. I am very willing to change anything about what I believe if given adequate reason to do so, and it is in every human's best interest to keep an open mind and do the same. How else can we ever learn and advance as individuals and as a society? I believe that a misunderstanding of how to disagree is the root cause of many problems in our society. It is what has created the culture of political correctness, and it stops us from being able to openly discuss what our true problems are, and thus stops us from searching for true solutions.

In fact, it is important to understand that it is impossible for society to progress if we do not have a means to disagree with each other. If all we do is passively exist around each other, agreeing or pretending to agree with the status quo, then nothing will change. The reason that we disagree is because we want to help improve each other's quality of life. If you see someone living a destructive lifestyle and you express your disagreement with their choices, then that will likely not be an easy conversation. But it is the only way to create positive social change, and so we do it because we care. This is the heart and soul of The Never Ending Brainstorm; that no one person has all the answers and only by working together can we reveal the truth.

Growing up, my father always told me he didn't want problem people, but solution people. Bringing up a problem is saying that the computer doesn't work. Bringing up a solution is saying that the data cable from the PC to the monitor isn't working, and replacing it will bring back functionality. The difference is that one solves nothing and causes worry, and the other is actionable and brings relief. That mentality has stuck with me my entire life, and that is the way that the problems I see in our society will be presented and solved.

There are three root problems for all of the struggles in our country; (1) The vast over complication of the law, (2) a substantial drift from the concept of a "Representative" Democracy, and (3) a substantial drift from the concept of a "Representative Democracy." Once these three problems are corrected, it will become very clear how problems such as homelessness, crime, starvation, and inefficient government systems can be easily corrected as well.

Obviously, the over complication of the law has one

of the most significant consequences for society. We have come to a point in which there is not a single person who knows every single law. Even laws that are well-known are written with unnecessarily complex language. What this means, then, is that every single citizen is perpetually at risk of committing crimes that they did not even know were crimes. This is no way to go through life, and stems from a misunderstanding about what laws are supposed to be. We as a people must come together and agree to the idea of a government in order to protect ourselves from certain things.

Don't want to get murdered? Fine, but you have to agree not to murder anyone. Don't want to get robbed? Fine, but you have to agree not to rob anyone. Every single law that requires something of you as a citizen should have some direct benefit to you as well. If it does not, then that law needs to be seriously reconsidered. Unfortunately, though, that is not the way that our system has been set up to evolve. Instead, the system in our country that creates laws essentially just empowers our financial elite to make changes as they see fit. The second and third problems are intertwined in a lot of ways, but it's crucial to understand them as separate as well. We have drifted from the concept of a Representative Democracy, in both senses of the term.

First and foremost, our representatives no longer represent us. This is not to blame any politicians directly, but rather that the system has naturally evolved this way and, as we know, people are a product of their environments. This is because the election process is no longer a fair process. Rather than having a true representative sample of the population, we are forced to choose between two people who come from the same minority population: the financial elite. An oligarchy is a system in which a small group of people are given the power to make laws, and that is exactly what our country has become.

The second aspect that makes our system non-democratic is the way in which lobbying and potential corruption have evolved. The word "potential" here is important, because we are not so much worried with whether or not any politician in particular has ever been potentially corrupt, but rather that the system allows for that potential at all. Removing that potential is the only way to correct the problem, otherwise we are just churning more well-intentioned people through a system that allows them the opportunity to abuse their power.

When addressing the solutions to these problems, it is important to avoid two things: overly complex solutions and solutions that don't

> *If we simultaneously tweak every flawed element in the system, it is possible to create solutions without the detrimental side effects.*

reach far enough. Overcomplicating things is an obvious problem; if people cannot understand the solution they are likely unwilling to accept it. The lack of comprehensiveness is a problem because of the complexity in our current system. There are so many spinning gears and moving parts, that trying to fix one at a time usually creates other unforeseeable problems in other areas. However, if we simultaneously tweak every flawed element in the system, it is possible to create solutions without the detrimental side effects, and that is exactly my intention.

If there is anything about what you just read that you do not agree with, or do not understand, or if you want to hear about some of the proposed social solutions to our problems, I urge you to read the full text of The Never Ending Brainstorm. If you still are unsure after that, or even if you are sure that these solutions will not work and you know why, then please contact me and let me know so we can work together to create true positive social change. Only by disagreeing with each other appropriately can we come to the truth of how to solve our problems together.

PART 1: THE ORGANIZATION OF THOUGHT

Preparing Our Minds for Change

LOGIC AND THE SCIENTIFIC METHOD

It may seem odd to start a book on social and political change with a discussion about how to think and what thinking is, but nothing could be more important. If a hospital was staffed entirely by doctors with illnesses, it wouldn't matter how incredible the hospital was, it would always inevitably fail. The same is true of our society; if the people are not prepared to think critically and understand each other, then no amount of change will help.

Our world is rapidly straying from logic as we see more and more emotionally charged information than objectively stated information. Logic and science are crucial in the pursuit of knowledge and the pursuit of truth, because they allow the same experiments (or the same patterns of thought) to be replicated by anyone around the world and achieve the same results. Otherwise, we could all run rampant claiming our own "truths" and there would be no way to counter it.

The systems of logic and science give us a framework to

The systems of logic and science give us a framework to decide if what we are hearing is an opinion, a fact, a theory, or just wrong.

19

decide if what we are hearing is an opinion, a fact, a theory, or just wrong. A New Yorker article describes it as "a system that corrects for people's natural inclinations. In a well-run laboratory, there's no room for myside bias; the results have to be reproducible in other laboratories, by researchers who have no motive to confirm them. And this, it could be argued, is why the system has proved so successful. At any given moment, a field may be dominated by squabbles, but, in the end, the methodology prevails" (Kolbert, 2017).

> *The mass misunderstanding of why it is important to be intentionally rational in our thoughts is the root of many of the problems our society faces.*

The mass misunderstanding of why it is important to be intentionally rational in our thoughts is the root of many of the problems our society faces. Therefore, it is critical to have an understanding of logic when beginning the journey towards The Never Ending Brainstorm. Logic is simply an organized set of principles that allow us as intelligent beings to interact. It is the foundation of all human conversation and thought. Logic is simply the mathematics of ideas. We all should strive to have our ideas and beliefs founded in logic.

The details of logic can be very complicated, but the foundation is quite simple. Logic is a tool for determining if a particular thought is valid. There are some fundamental principles, as well as a list of logical fallacies, which are simply mistakes that you should not make. The law of identity says, "whatever is, is," the law of non-contradiction says, "nothing can both be and not be," and the law of excluded middle says, "everything must be or not be" (Britannica). In essence, every thought is either valid or not, and cannot be both or neither. If this seems like common sense so far, that's because it is, and logic really should be mostly common sense.

Logical fallacies are probably the most important part to remember, because it really is just a list of mistakes that people make and need to avoid making. The Ad Hominem fallacy is when you respond to an argument by attacking the person's character, which is obviously irrelevant to the merit of the point being made. The Appeal to Authority fallacy is when someone makes the mistake of assuming something is true just because an authority figure represented it. The fallacies of Composition and Division are when you assume that what is true of the whole is true of a part, or that what is true of a part is true of the whole. There are dozens of other fallacies that should be studied to avoid, but most often, if you think about an issue long enough, you will start to notice the fallacies without even having to name them because those ways of thinking just don't make sense.

The scientific method builds upon logic. The main difference between the scientific method and logic is that logic can be used to discuss hypothetical situations, where the scientific method can only be used to discuss observable and measurable situations. Whenever possible, when discussing an idea, one should always attempt to use the scientific method to prove or disprove an idea. Only when direct observation is impossible should logic be used without any scientific methodology behind it.

Unfortunately, the scientific method is often used incorrectly. It is usually thought of as a way to prove things true, and that could not be more wrong. A hypothesis, the start of any scientific endeavor, is simply a potential answer to any question you want to know. When forming this hypothesis, you will always use logic to come up with your best potential answer before starting in on your actual experimentation.

The scientific method is a means of attempting to disprove a hypothesis, and only when every possible means

> *When you have an idea, you should try to poke as many holes as possible in that idea yourself before you bring it in front of other people.*

of invalidation are exhausted, then a hypothesis can become a theory. This shift in mentality makes a massive difference when it comes to creating a defense for an idea that may or may not be immediately accepted at face value.

Using the scientific method is actually very simple. All you need to start out with is a question. What is it about the world that you want to know? Once you have a question, it is time to do some digging and see if others have researched the same subject in a logical and scientific manner. Perhaps someone has done a study that you could replicate or expand upon. This is the opportunity to look for weaknesses in other research strategies so you can avoid them in your own.

Once your idea is articulated, your only job is to prove yourself wrong. Do everything you can to prove yourself wrong. Coincidentally, this same concept also applies to the practice of logic. When you have an idea, you should try to poke as many holes as possible in that idea yourself before you bring it in front of other people. Only once you have

23

exhausted every means of disproving your hypothesis, then it can be accepted as valid, at least until a more convincing hypothesis comes along. Just like an architect designing a house, testing all potential problems and ensuring they do not exist is the only way to guarantee the product's final success.

> *It is the nature of humanity to overburden ourselves with complexity, so it is our duty to counteract that by striving for simplicity.*

Finally, the concept of Occam's Razor enables us to select the most logical choices. Occam asserted that whenever there are two conflicting hypotheses, the one that requires the least amount of assumptions should be accepted as correct. The simpler an explanation, the more likely it is to be true.

It is the nature of humanity to overburden ourselves with complexity, so it is our duty to counteract that by striving for simplicity. Thus, if logic is truly the foundation of our thoughts and interactions, we should attempt to use it in our lives as often as possible, especially when it comes to interacting with others and with society. The mass acceptance and understanding of a logical approach to life is foundational to the changes that society drastically needs.

APPLYING LOGIC TO LIFE

All of this is great in theory, but putting it to use is the hard part. There are a few fundamentals that everyone seems to forget, and then there are some things that many people seem to have never considered. We all need to be approaching life with a student mentality. The moment you decide that you have it all figured it out is the moment you stop really living. Every day is a new opportunity to learn new things and grow as a person. Every interaction with another person is a chance to learn from them and to help them learn.

We also often forget that not everyone knows what we know, which can cause us to become frustrated with them, when really, we should be excited to share whatever information it is

> *We all need to be approaching life with a student mentality. The moment you decide that you have it all figured it is the moment you stop really living.*

that we have. In every situation with another person, if you can try to put yourself in their shoes and see through their eyes, it becomes much easier to communicate effectively.

Beyond these core ideas, what it comes down to is a

change in the way that we have conversations. Every conversation that has ever taken place on earth falls into one of three categories: entertainment, agreement, or disagreement. Obviously, this is a mass simplification; most conversations have multiple if not all of these elements, plus many others. However, when listening to someone, your mind will naturally fall into one of these three states based upon the topic of conversation. We as humans are very good at two of these; it is not difficult to entertain or be entertained, nor is it particularly challenging to agree with someone or to be agreed with. What we often struggle with is how to properly disagree with each other, which is unfortunate because it is without a doubt the most important part because it is how we grow.

Social change is inevitable. The world today is different from the world just 10 years ago, which is different from the world 100 years before that, and 10 years from now the world will be a very different place again. That is not to say that all change is good; one look at a history book will tell us that it is very easy to change for the worse. Not all change is progress, but all progress is change, and if change is

> *Not all change is progress, but all progress is change, and if change is inevitable then a structured forum for change should be a required part of any advancing society.*

inevitable then a structured forum for change should be a required part of any advancing society. Entertainment and agreement cannot create change; one is passive and the other protects the status quo, which is not always a bad thing. However, only disagreement has the potential to create change. This is why a culture of political correctness is so dangerous; because it limits the ways people are able to disagree and therefore limits the extent to which society can advance.

What we need to do, then, is to change the way that we as people disagree with each other. Many like to form their opinions as a solid and put them in a box. Whenever they discuss these ideas with others, they view the disagreement as "my idea versus your idea" in a combative sense. Discussions end with a clear winner and loser, with one idea being right and one idea being wrong. This is in part what created the culture of political correctness that we see today, where people get offended over seemingly trivial issues. Unfortunately, the fault often lies with both parties;

29

the offender and the offended.

The answer to this is quite simple and relies only on a change in mentality. When we enter discussions, it should not be a matter of idea versus idea. Rather, it should be a collective search for the best idea currently available. An understanding that both parties are likely to be partially right, and partially wrong. What it becomes from there is math: my idea + your idea - logical fallacies = the truth.

My idea
+
your idea
−
logical fallacies
=
the truth.

An easy example is if you and a friend were discussing the health benefits of caffeine. You go in saying that caffeine is a great metabolism booster, and your friend argues that it is a cardiovascular irritant. If you go in combatively, neither person will gain anything from the discussion. But if you enter the discussion with this positive mentality, then you will both learn that in moderation, caffeine is good for you, but in excess, it can be dangerous.

When you are sharing your opinion with someone, do so with the understanding that their thoughts on it may be cause to change it. When someone presents their opinion to you, do not poke holes in it maliciously, but with the intention of helping them to strengthen their own point of view. In fact, it is often of huge benefit to acknowledge this understanding prior to entering a discussion. If opinions and beliefs are viewed as fluid, rather than solid, then adopting new truths as they are discovered allows an opinion to always be valid. Only by living in constant truth can this type of validity be achieved in a set of beliefs. This is the heart and soul of The Never Ending Brainstorm; that no one person has all the answers and only by working together can we achieve the truth.

When you are sharing your opinion with someone, do so with the understanding that their thoughts on it may be cause to change it.

After all, this is how science operates, so why should individuals not strive to operate the same way? It was accepted as fact that the sun revolved around the earth until we discovered otherwise, then that fact changed. It was socially accepted that the earth was flat until that was proved untrue, and then the scientific community

No one person has all the answers and only by working together can we achieve the truth.

progressed. But when it comes to social and political issues, people have a much harder time being logical because government decisions about civil rights can have a heavy impact on human emotion.

All of this, and then you add in to the mix the abundance of bad science and overhyped media, and it can be very hard for the average person to decipher what is right and wrong. As cognizant beings, however, it is our duty to identify these weaknesses in our own psychology and do what we can to consciously overcome them. We need to be asking ourselves why certain issues make us emotional, and

> *It is our duty to identify these weaknesses in our own psychology and do what we can to consciously overcome them.*

why it hinders us from coming to the truth of the matter. All people should do everything they can to ensure that their beliefs and opinions are founded in logic as much as possible.

PHILOSOPHY, RELIGION, AND SCIENCE

Science and philosophy have never been at odds, rather, they are complimenting systems. The definitive concept of philosophy encompasses all types of belief systems and ways of life, including religions. If science deals only with the observable universe, then philosophy takes over where the point of observation ends. The most defensible philosophies, worldviews, and religions are the ones that are founded in logic.

This is where being able to distinguish good science from false science is important. Understanding the relationship and differences between science and all the

> *The most defensible philosophies, worldviews, and religions are the ones that are founded in logic.*

belief systems of the world is important because it is one of the most heavily debated conversation topics. If we are striving to improve our ability to disagree effectively, then this should also be understood on a broad scale.

Many people have tried to say that science has disproved the existence of a deity, and unfortunately that just isn't how science works. It is obvious that there is a significant lack of physical proof of a higher power of any kind, but that does not disprove it. Instead, that simply means that the discussion of the possibility of a higher power does not lie with the scientific method. Instead, it belongs to the world of logical thought.

Fortunately, the logical/philosophical community has come to some sort of an answer on the subject; although the answer comes in the form of a problem. While the existence of a higher power (i.e. God/gods, karma, etc.) cannot be scientifically proven at this point in time, the point of view that there is no higher power is tough to defend because it faces a logical fallacy known as infinite regress. The fallacy basically entails maintaining a point of view that requires an infinitely stacking set of assumptions. If A came from B, where did B come from? If B came from C, where did C come from?

If we look at our own physical universe, one is forced to accept one of the following options. Either the rules of nature we currently accept as fact are incorrect, or something exists outside of the rules of nature that we know. Many practicing religious people believe in the big bang, because plenty of religious texts describe something similar to the big bang, such as in the creation story told in Genesis.

> *Debating philosophical or religious ideas will take a lot of careful treading. Just as your individual religion cannot currently be disproved by science, it also cannot currently be proven true by science.*

Even still, the question remains of what caused the big bang? If it was two colliding particles in a vacuum, where did those particles come from? If we continue to ask the questions backwards, the conclusion remains that either something created itself, which defies the laws of energy conservation, or that something has existed infinitely backwards in time, which would require a power beyond that of our physical universe as well.

This is the reason that many scientists also practice religion personally. If science had really methodologically disproven the existence of a god, wouldn't there be an overwhelming majority of scientists who held those beliefs in their own lives? In fact, a worldwide study on religion and science found that more than half of scientists worldwide self-identify as "religious" and saw no conflict between science and religion (McCaig). What this means, however, is that debating philosophical or religious ideas will take a lot of careful treading. Just as your individual religion cannot currently be disproved by science, it also cannot currently be proven true by science. This is why it is so important to be tolerant to other ways of life. From a practical point of view, as long as a religion preaches peace and tolerance, it does not matter what the hypothetical afterlife situation is.

HARD SCIENCES VERSUS SOFT SCIENCES

A major point of misunderstanding about science in our society is in the difference between hard sciences and soft sciences. The lack of understanding about this important difference is a major factor in many of the social problems we see today. A struggling education system, a prison system that creates more criminals than it eliminates, a severe misunderstanding and false categorization of mental illnesses, and many other problems all stem from this simple split in the world of science. Hard sciences include mathematics, chemistry, physics, and biology, while soft sciences include psychology, anthropology, political science and sociology.

These two sides to science are named based on the type of data that each one deals with. In the hard sciences, data is concrete. Two hydrogen and one oxygen will always create H_2O, or water. Acceleration due to gravity always increases at a rate of 9.80665 meters per second squared. In the soft sciences, this is not the case. You cannot say

> *In the hard sciences, data is concrete... In the soft sciences, this is not the case.*

conclusively that all white people are democrats, or that everyone with bipolar disorder (BPD) will own a minivan. With the proper research, it might be possible to say that being white makes you 70% more likely to vote democrat, or that data shows minivan owners to have BPD with an 85% confidence interval, but never conclusive facts.

The problem with this is that it leaves a lot up to interpretation, and a many scientists believe it is their place to attempt to do that interpreting. This is where the age-old adage "correlation does not equal causation" comes from. Just because 85% of people who own minivans have BPD does not mean that having BPD causes you to buy a minivan, or that buying a minivan causes BPD. It is possible that it is one or the other, or that they are unrelated, or that it is one of many factors influencing the other. The important thing is being able to read the data itself and being able to make your own inferences about what you are reading.

> *Correlation does not equal causation... The important thing is being able to read the data itself and being able to make your own inferences about what you are reading.*

A perfect example of this misunderstanding is with the correlation between video games and real world violence. For a long time it was thought that video games could cause violence, and there seemed to be data that backed it up. However, more modern studies are controlling for factors such as family history and predisposition towards violence. A study at Western Michigan University did just that and found the link between violence and video games to be statistically insignificant, and a study done by the Southern Economic Administration actually found that violence within cities was inversely correlated to the sales of violent video games (Scutti).

Of course, these correlations need to be studied further to fully understand if there is a cathartic effect to video games, and if they can increase a predisposition to violence, and when which one is appropriate. This is analogous to the concept of a single beer to an alcoholic versus a single beer to someone without an addiction. Many people, however, are not willing to read into the details to understand what it means, and would rather just ban video games entirely. The answer here is obvious, though, in that parents just need to get to know their kids and understand that what is appropriate for one child may not be for another.

This applies on a broader scale as well. Our school system needs to understand what makes kids want to learn, and not just blindly read at the students out of a book or off a presentation. Our prison management system needs

> *It is also crucial that we understand logic and the scientific method at the individual level, because these practices are the foundations of almost everything we discuss.*

to look at why people make the choices they make before and after coming to jail, and how to keep people out. Our government leadership needs to understand what makes its citizens do what they do, and how to keep people happy, employed, and motivated. Understanding the difference between hard and soft sciences is crucial to this undertaking, because only then can we understand how to apply the results of the research done in those fields to real life.

It is also crucial that we understand logic and the scientific method at the individual level, because these practices are the foundations of almost everything we discuss. We have all had those moments in conversations where someone just wasn't understanding the point, and we have all been on the other side of that as well. Sometimes it is because the idea being explained just isn't correct or isn't being explained correctly, and sometimes it is because the person hearing it doesn't have the proper logical processes to internalize it correctly. In both cases, all of our lives would be improved daily by a mass education of logic and the scientific method.

PART 2: THE ORIGINS OF SOCIETAL FLAWS

Understanding the Past to Shape the Future

THE EVOLUTION OF POLITICAL FLAWS

Societies do not just form on their own, and political systems are not created at random. There is a natural state of humanity that exists only with the law of nature, and the path to forming human law is quite interesting. John Locke, considered to be one of the founding fathers of political science, discusses this idea in his Second Treatise on Government. His ideas may be a bit outdated, and rudimentary due to the fact that they were some of the first recorded ideas on the topic, but they form the foundation for almost all of political ideology and are worth reading on their own.

In nature, man is free to do as he pleases. In laymen's terms, this political system is known as anarchy. Every person can lie, cheat, steal, and murder with no law to inhibit them, but that also means that they may be lied to, cheated, robbed or murdered at any time without any promise of retribution. At some point, groups of people who find themselves interacting regularly may come together and agree upon a basic set of rules. From this point onwards, every law that is made is a trade. Each individual gives up one of their "rights,"

> *Each individual gives up one of their "rights," and in exchange the society as a whole gets protection related to what was given up.*

and in exchange the society as a whole gets protection related to what was given up. It starts out with giving up the right to murder and steal in exchange for the protection from being murdered or stolen from.

For example, education is mandatory for all children living in the United States. Americans give up the freedom of being able to choose whether or not to educate their children, and in exchange we all collectively get the benefit of an at least partially educated society. Most would agree that is an excellent trade. In modern times, the Patriot Act is a perfect example of such a trade. American citizens gave up their right to go through airports quickly and easily in exchange for the notion that our airways would be safer. The problem with these types of tradeoffs is in knowing where the cutoff point is. How far do we lean towards security or how far do we lean towards personal freedom? This is why issues such as gun control, abortion, and immigration have always been such points of contention.

The type of government is equally important in

determining the success of the society. Governments are simply defined by what segment of the population makes the rules. If only one person makes the rules, it is a monarchy. If a minority group of some kind makes the rules, then it is an oligarchy. And if the entire society is involved in making the rules, it is a democracy. Each of these governments can take different forms.

A good monarch is a king, and a bad one is a tyrant. An oligarchy could be a theocracy (rule by religion), an aristocracy (rule by the elite), or a financial oligarchy (a rule by the rich). Democracy might manifest itself as representative democracy, or as a direct democracy. Being able to tell the difference between different forms of government is important in understanding what factors motivate the decision makers.

Many people view the government as a separate entity; some faraway concept as something to be feared and not trusted. When something makes decisions that impact daily life in major ways, it is natural to have a healthy respect for that type of power. And when that power makes

> *How far do we lean towards security or how far do we lean towards personal freedom?*

consistent decisions that impact people's lives in a negative way, the very same respect can turn into

> *Awareness of the purpose of your government is vital to the continual pursuit of improving its effectiveness.*

fear. While it is possible for a government to evolve into this type of monstrosity, this is not what a government is by nature. By nature, a government is simply a social contract between all citizens of the land. Awareness of the purpose of your government is vital to the continual pursuit of improving its effectiveness.

THE EVOLUTION OF ECONOMIC FLAWS

Interestingly enough, money is also a part of this social contract. It is easy to think of money as just another resource, but it is important to be able to distinguish between true resources and money. Just like it is hard for us in today's age to conceptualize a world without rules and order, it is also tough to think about what a world without money looks like. But that world existed as well, and at one point people either produced everything they needed or they had to trade for it. At a certain point, however, trading becomes inefficient. The guy who has cows wants lumber, but the guy who owns the lumber yard doesn't want milk or steak. Do we bring in a third, unrelated party to make a three way trade? Eventually, people will agree something can act as a representative of value for both goods and time value of services.

This has taken many different forms throughout the ages. Gold, diamonds, jewels, coins, paper money, promissory notes, even salt at one time. That's right, for a long while certain societies used salt as money. You got paid in salt by weight, and when you wanted to buy something you went out with your bag of salt to trade for whatever it

> *Now, money is simply backed by good faith in the government, and the vast majority of it exists electronically.*

was that you wanted. This system actually worked pretty well, because unlike money, salt has actual value, not just conceptual value. You can actually use salt for a tangible purpose in your life.

This is the exact same reason that for centuries, the US dollar was backed by the gold standard. Every bank had gold in the vault, and money had an actual physical object backing it. Now, money is simply backed by good faith in the government, and the vast majority of it exists electronically.

What gets people confused about money is in thinking that it's limited. It is not. The government prints money every year and will continue to do so until the end of time. This makes sense, of course, as new people are entering the system at the same time as well. What is necessary, then, is a system that has enough money in it to support the growing population within that particular government. This is a bit of a false problem too, however, as the problem is money movement, not money quantity.

A single dollar bill could hypothetically perform every transaction that takes place in the world today, given that it could move quickly enough. Obviously, in the real world money does not move this quickly, so what needs to be understood is the balance between allowing money movement to account for new members of society and adding new money to the system as new citizens are added. For a long time, the policy was trickle-down economics. If the rich and the business owners have the money, then that should hypothetically allow them to hire more people and pump more money into the system. The science of it, however, shows the opposite to be the case.

For as long as we have been tracking it, money trickles up, not down. The rich continue to get richer, the poor become more numerous and the middle class is slowly edged out. An independent study by the Center on Budget and Policy Priorities found that this gap has increased even more than usual over the last 20 years (Stone). Sure, there are lots of "assistance" programs, but their success rates are dismal and more often than not are simply taken

> *For as long as we have been tracking it, money trickles up, not down. The rich continue to get richer, the poor become more numerous and the middle class is slowly edged out.*

advantage of. Every other policy related to money seems to just push it further to the top.

If we were to give a million dollars to every person in America, within one year 90% of that money would be in the hands of the wealthy and the business owners. This is because we have a system that does not protect free market capitalism, but monopolized capitalism. Add in the political system of lobbying and financial backing for campaigns, and it is easy to see how the system got that way. No one person is to blame, however. Our society and economic structure have been set up like a game. There are rules to this game, and there are clear winners and clear losers. We cannot blame the winners for winning at the game, but perhaps it is time for a new game.

> *We cannot blame the winners for winning at the game, but perhaps it is time for a new game.*

PART 3: CHANGES TO MODERN SOCIETY

Bringing the Brainstorm to Life

EDUCATION REFORM

Before it is possible to dive into the concept of societal and political reform, the system of education in our society must be addressed. Creating a working system and then putting improperly trained people and in that system has the potential to break it. Once we are able to properly foster students from childhood into functioning members of society, only then can we create a social and political structure that allows us to achieve our full potential, individually and collectively. There are two major problems with the education system today; the goal of the system, and the method used to reinforce information retention.

First and foremost, the goal of the education system must be properly aligned before a method can begin to even be discussed. If we do not know where we are going, how can we hope to get there? Just

> *Once we are able to properly bring up students from childhood into functioning members of society, only then can we create a social and political structure that allows us to achieve our full potential, individually and collectively.*

> *The central focus of education should be to create functioning members of society that are not only able to think critically on their own, but be able to peacefully disagree with others in order to get a better understanding of the world.*

about anywhere in the US, you will see teaching for test grades. Government funding of schools is in part based upon the standardized testing students participate in, and so the staff puts pressure on the teachers to ensure good grades of the students. In turn, the instructors wind up teaching not for true material comprehension, but to be able to pass a standardized test. The central focus of education should be to create functioning members of society that are not only able to think critically on their own, but be able to peacefully disagree with others in order to get a better understanding of the world.

In order to do this, a couple of methodological changes need to take place. The largest of these is emphasizing the importance of applying logic and science to every aspect of life. If these two concepts are the means by which we are supposed to break down and analyze the world, then should that not be the primary focus? There needs to be regular emphasis put on these subjects all throughout elementary school as the foundation for all other subjects that are taught. This, along with a general education around mathematics, science (soft and hard), the arts, and physical education should make up the majority of elementary school.

These years should also be relatively non-stressful. Kids need plenty of time to play, and school should be something that they look forward to. There should be little to no homework, as most of the learning will be happening at school. One important concept to remember here is that teachers should teach about a subject, not teach a subject. Teaching math is telling someone that 2 plus 2 equals 4. Teaching about math is telling them that there are thousands of potential formulas for solving any number of potential problems involving numbers, and getting them excited about how to apply that in their everyday life.

Finland is a perfect example of where this has worked. They jumped from being ranked below average in education to having one of the top ranked education systems in the world simply by implementing a few of these solutions (D'Orio). It isn't necessarily easy, as Finland had economic and social factors that aided in this process, but it is definitely a goal to strive towards.

By the time children are hitting puberty and entering junior high, they should have a general understanding of the way the world works. They can read and write, and understand basic science, math, psychology and the core of our political structure. There should be an emphasis placed on understanding how necessities are provided for, like food, water, shelter, and protection. Maslow's Hierarchy of Needs should be at the forefront of everyone's minds when considering the needs of society. They should also know the basics of other societal necessities, such as the

transportation, legal, journalism, and entertainment industries. Most importantly, students should start to look at where their strengths play best in a working society and start to hone those skills towards something that is both enjoyable and beneficial.

Last but not least, the classroom environment needs a major makeover. The current method is not particularly

> *Students should start to look at where their strengths play best in a working society and start to hone those skills towards something that is both enjoyable and beneficial.*

successful; lecturing students only serves to disengage and bore them. This causes the majority of information to be lost. In the professional world, a similar phenomena is seen; the phrase "Death by PowerPoint" refers to the notion that PowerPoint presentations are not efficient nor effective in teaching people new things. This boils down to one of those general misunderstandings about social sciences. In fact, we have figured out the most effective method for teaching and it is simply not being utilized in most schools.

People tend to remember about 10% of what they read, 20% of what they hear, 30% of what they see, 80% of what they experience and 90% of what they teach to

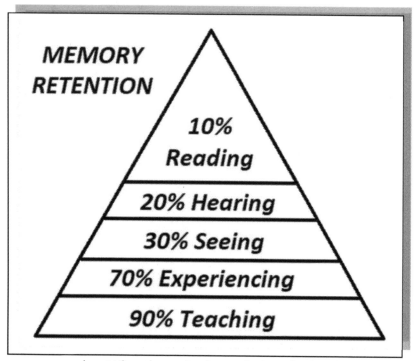

MEMORY RETENTION

10% Reading

20% Hearing

30% Seeing

70% Experiencing

90% Teaching

someone else. Why, then, do the majority of schools use the weakest three of the means? A truly effective teaching environment looks very different from just reading, listening and watching. Instead of rigorous class schedules, each classroom should have a focus topic and be an open learning environment like a lab. Students will be encouraged to go where they feel the most need, whether that is to hone a strength or to explore an area of weakness. Students can be graded on both their achievements in these labs and on their ability to teach the younger students, which will be heavily encouraged. This concept, called "interteaching," is well known and understood in the psychology (Saville).

In many cases, post high school education is not a requirement. There has been a constant societal pressure on our youth to attend college, whether they need to or not for what their goals are in life. A K-12 education should be enough to get a job in most professions, because it should have taught the students how to categorize and retrieve information, rather than just to memorize and regurgitate it. This will allow people to continue learning new things easily and successfully throughout their lives, rather than just being pigeonholed into whatever they feel is right for them at a certain time.

> *A K-12 education should be enough to get a job in most professions, because it should have taught the students how to categorize and retrieve information, rather than just to memorize and regurgitate it.*

A thriving education system is the most important step in societal advancement. Without it, all the political and economic change in the world will fall to waste as the uneducated constituents run it into the ground.

Logic and the scientific method are the building blocks for all of our ideas, so creating that as the foundation for future generations is the best thing that can be done for them. A society where children are trained from an early age to listen and respect other people's ideas, but also to think critically about them and be willing to challenge them, is the society that will advance faster than any other.

POLITICAL REFORM

The American political system is one of the best governments in place right now, but there is substantial room for improvement. When our country was founded, it was founded on the idea that every citizen is equal under the law. What "equal" means and how that phrase is interpreted, however, is the point of much contention. We all have our own version of how a perfect society looks. If you controlled the whole world, what would that perfect society look like?

While this exercise is both fun and meaningful, it does not translate well to real life applicability. So rather than painting a picture of a perfect political and economic system, it is more efficient to simply look at the shortcomings of the current system, and draw a path to correcting the issues that are identified. It is important to be able to identify the real issues, because only treating the symptoms often allows them to return.

> *it is more efficient to simply look at the shortcomings of the current system, and draw a path to correcting the issues that are identified.*

The first and most prominent issue in our political system is the excessive level of complexity it creates. Not only is each law itself written in overly complex language, but there are so many laws that no one person can ever know them all, whether federal, state, or local. There are even joke books and websites dedicated to the thousands of ridiculous laws still on the books.

What this means is that any person in the United States, at any given time, is potentially at risk of committing a crime that they didn't know was

> *How can people be expected to follow the law when they don't fully know it?*

against the law. It is no wonder that much of the population treat the police force with caution, rather than feeling safe when they are around. How can people be expected to follow the law when they don't fully know it?

Referring back to the evolution of society, a government originally evolves as a tool of agreement and disagreement between people. The law, then, should be very common sense as it really should only inhibit the citizens from harming or suppressing other citizens. And even if a law may not necessarily be understood by common sense, it should at least be easily accessible and easily understandable

74

by anyone affected by it. Fortunately, the issue of accessibility is at least already being solved by the increased prominence of information technology in our lives. What we need to do is fully maximize the potential of the most interconnected society this world has ever had to create a better world for ourselves and future generations.

Technology is creating more opportunity in so many different ways that it is impossible to mention them all. Possibly the most powerful opportunity is the concept of a countrywide or even global forum. Already there are websites set up like this, although none are government-based. Interestingly enough, the very first recorded instance of democracy in history utilized a country wide forum for decision making, both legislative and judicial.

Granted, the Athenian Democracy had a much smaller population then. Population expansion was part of the reason it eventually failed, but it still lasted two centuries. For over 2000 years after that, the concept of a direct democracy sat dormant

> *What we need to do is fully maximize the potential of the most interconnected society this world has ever had to create a better world for ourselves and future generations.*

due primarily to the impossibility of gathering all citizens of a country to make decisions. Only in the past century has this type of communication become real.

Obviously, the Athenian Democracy model is a bit of "utopian dreaming," and would be next to impossible to implement in this country. However, the concept of true democracy is something we can strive toward, and there are some pretty significant yet simple to perform changes that we can make to align ourselves with our true values. Our "Representative Democracy" has turned into more of a "Financial Oligarchy." The United States government meets the dictionary definition of an oligarchy, which was studied in great detail at Princeton University (Mass).

Originally, the idea was that anyone could run for office, and then those who made it into office would be the only ones both to debate and to vote on the laws. Now, however, thanks to the increased necessity for exorbitant campaign costs, only the already financially elite make it into office. It is important to keep in mind that there are no individuals to blame for the way this system has evolved. We don't hate

> *Our "Representative Democracy" has turned into more of a "Financial Oligarchy."*

any of the players, but the game sure needs a few changes.

The first and most obvious is to eliminate the massive campaign costs and simplify the campaign process significantly. It is understandable that in a world without technology, the need would exist for hiring tons of people and printing tons of banners and t-shirts and all other costs associated. The solution for this problem also solves the problem of the two-party system, which our founding fathers warned us against.

> *Eliminate the massive campaign costs and simplify the campaign process significantly.*

John Adams said, "There is nothing which I dread so much as a division of the republic into two great parties, each arranged under its leader, and concerting measures in opposition to each other. This, in my humble apprehension, is to be dreaded as the greatest political evil under our Constitution." George Washington was quick to agree, in a speech that is much too long to include but is definitely worth a read.

Campaign periods need to be shortened and advertising needs to be legislated out of the picture. To make things simple, a series of speeches and debates will be what citizens will have to decide from. Social media will continue to play a role, because that is one of the fairest public forums that exists. Anyone can comment, anyone can post, and anyone can see. Obviously, there will need to be a scale of intensity of the campaign periods based upon what level of government the position is at. So, an election for mayor may last a few weeks and have only a few speeches and debates, a presidential election could last 3 months and have dozens of these publicly broadcasted events. In fact, many other democratic nations have much shorter election cycles than the United States, thanks to laws keeping them from getting out of hand (Kurtzleben).

Doing away with the party system entirely, the primary election would consist of any individual who could get a pre-determined number of nominations from the constituents. They would all be given a chance to give one or a number of speeches before a first round election would come up with the top candidates. From there, the real campaigning and debating would begin, and one final election (and potentially a runoff) would determine the candidate. At this point, voting should be something that can be conveniently managed electronically.

On the topic of voting electronically, all of these campaign changes don't necessarily solve the complex problems our government faces. Once people are in office, lobbying still allow laws to be potentially determined by the best interest of corporations rather than the individuals the government officials are supposed to be representing. Even if you don't believe that bribery or corruption takes place, just the possibility of that happening should be enough cause to take a closer look at what the decision making process in this country is and how our laws are really made. While a full Athenian Democracy would be an interesting social experiment using the internet as a forum, the vast majority of people would likely not actively participate in it.

> *Once people are in office, lobbying still allow laws to be potentially determined by the best interest of corporations rather than the individuals the government officials are supposed to be representing.*

Instead, the best middle ground is to leave the power of writing, debating, and editing bills to the elected representatives. The only change would be to utilize the same web based voting that is used for the election, and let the people vote on the law itself. This would take place after all the currently existing procedures, including the legislative vote and the executive signature. Not only would this eliminate the distraction of corporate involvement, but also forces the drafter of the bill to use language that can be easily understood. If a law is written in an overly complicated manner, people will vote against it simply because people will not want laws applying to them that cannot even be understood.

This concept, also coupled with the restructuring of the election process, should rebalance power to the citizens and away from incumbents. If an official were to go back on their election promises, or write arbitrary and confusing laws, the current system leaves us stuck with an election consisting of that incumbent and one potential newcomer. In this new system, the voice of the people is given to whoever is able to consistently articulate and execute the will of the constituents.

Along the lines of simplification, there also needs to be a concerted effort to remove old laws as new ones are created, preferably removed faster than created. It seems as though some sort of government

> *The voice of the people is given to whoever is able to consistently articulate and execute the will of the constituents.*

> *It isn't that people don't want to get involved with the government, it is primarily that people feel their contribution is insignificant and because it isn't currently convenient.*

based application needs to be created to house all of this information. After all, why not? Most people already trust their entire financial and personal information to either a web based or phone based app, or both. It makes sense then, that you should have some sort of "account" to be able to do business with the government.

Based on your login info, it would have lists of all the applicable laws: federal, state, and local. It would tell you what elections were coming up, what bills are coming up to be voted on, and would have links to a live stream of the debates going on by the elected representatives. It isn't that people don't want to get involved with the government, it is primarily that people feel their contribution is insignificant and because it isn't currently convenient. If it were made simple to do and people felt like their contribution mattered, they would be more likely to stay interested.

Right now, many people think of the government as some faraway entity that makes autonomous decisions and is to be feared. These changes would reignite the understanding that the government is just all of us together. Nothing says it better than the preamble to the Constitution of this great country. Not only does it very specifically point out that *we the people* are the ones who make it what it is, but it lays out the six purposes of the government. These must be held in the highest regard when debating and discussing new legislation, for they are both the foundation and the limit marks of what the government should do.

> *"We the People of the United States, in Order to form a more perfect Union, establish Justice, insure domestic Tranquility, provide for the common defense, promote the general Welfare, and secure the Blessings of Liberty to ourselves and our Posterity, do ordain and establish this Constitution for the United States of America."*

ECONOMIC REFORM

Changing the decision making process of the country is a strong first step towards solving our problems and creating an environment of equality for all, but it still leaves a great deal of unsolved problems. Homelessness, poverty, orphans, unemployment, prison recidivism, and mental health are all issues that still haunt our country. They seem to pop up everywhere in the media as well, and are extremely sensationalized. The issues are often not as bad as they seem, and some of the answers are already right in front of us. What it takes, first and foremost, is a new understanding of how our economy works and what the government's role is in it.

If money is a part of the social contract between people in a government, and if it is there as a collective representative of goods and services, then why is there an entire industry dedicated to profiting off it? Banks and credit agencies made sense in a world where money was a physical thing that had to be stored and moved, but the concept of storing money or getting a loan should always have simply been a branch of the government. And even if you don't believe that the financial industry is inherently a facet of the concept of government, the massive bailouts of the banks should have been treated as a purchase of the banks. After all, the U.S. Government is a corporation, with income and expenses, HR, everything a company has. Except instead of being the customers of the government, we are the

> *As equal share stockholders in the government, we need to start looking at what we want to "buy" and how we want our collective money to be spent.*

stockholders. As equal share stockholders in the government, we need to start looking at what we want to "buy" and how we want our collective money to be spent.

Many people get emotional over words without fully understanding the definitions. Capitalism and communism are two such words, and are often thought of as opposites. While this is somewhat true, it is more of a scale with each word on one end. An easier way to understand these concepts without the emotionally charged terms is to just call them individualism and collectivism. Every government is some kind of balance of these two things. A fully collectivist society is where everyone works for the state and

> *Every government is some kind of balance of capitalism and communism – or individualism and collectivism.*

is given an equal share, and a fully individualistic society is where nothing is provided by the government and everything must be produced or bought individually.

The goal, then, is to try to understand the strengths and weakness of these two concepts, and learn where they need to be applied. Some countries are "communist" in their education systems, or their healthcare, or even their Wi-Fi. In the United States, our "communism" is primarily a massive military, public education, some roadway and transportation funding, and scattered social programs such as food stamps and government housing.

If we are going to pick what we want to be "communist" about, then Maslow's Hierarchy of Needs should be the first place we start. On the topic of having everyone pitch in some (tax) and everyone get some (product/service), those things should be the things that every single person will always need, no matter what. One of the strengths of capitalism is that it encourages innovation in a developing field, like technology.

> *If we are going to pick what we want to be "communist" about, then Maslow's Hierarchy of Needs should be the first place we start.*

However, when there is little left to innovate, it can actually be harmful because the only way left to innovate is to hurt the product. Whether that is by trying to make the same final product using worse methods (like some of the changes in animal treatment in the food industry) or by designing intentional flaws to require customers to come back, capitalism has the potential both to hurt and to help.

All that being said, it is important that as industries are changed, no one's individual contributions will be devalued or lost. For example, in the government acquisition of the entire banking industry, no one has to lose their job or what they do, from the top all the way down to the bottom. In a standard corporate merger, it is not typical for one set of executives to be totally thrown off and a full assimilation begins. Rather, the executives of both corporations get together and discuss what works on one side, what works on the other, and come to a middle ground that maximizes the benefits of the new company as a whole.

So, all banks, from the massive powerhouses all the way down to the local banks could come together and form The Department of Banking. All local bankers will still keep their jobs, as people will still need the same level of interface. All that will change is the branding, the fees, and the transaction potential.

If all banks come under one roof, then there would only be need for one financial system. We the people would determine what loan types would be, what loan rates would be, and what fees (if any) would apply for what scenarios. Everyone would have full access to all of their money at any time, and transacting between accounts would be seamless and easily trackable. There are a few other hidden benefits to this assimilation of the financial industry.

> *It's not that there are not enough homes in this country, it is just that the people that need them aren't in them.*

The most important benefit is the list of assets that come along with the banking industry. Earlier, some problems were discussed such as homelessness and starvation. And while homelessness is a big problem, it is a bit of a false problem. It's not that there are not enough homes in this country, it is just that the people that need them aren't in them. Most studies put the rate as high as 6 to 1, meaning that there are six times as many emptied, foreclosed houses than there are homeless people to fill them (Bronson). Again, we cannot blame the bankers, there are some very well understood reasons why as a business you would not allow potential risks in the homes.

The same is true of starvation; many grocery stores and restaurants in this country throw away good food every day after reaching the shelf expiration, rather than give it to the needy like they do in many other countries. But it is often corporate policy; in a legal system where even a homeless person could sue for eating a bad donated piece of food, companies have to protect their interests. France was recently the first country to legislate against food waste, and the only issue they had was that charities did not have the capacity to handle all the food they were getting (Bryant).

Before we decide to just start giving away houses or even letting people live in them, we need to look at the psychology behind homelessness and poverty to understand how to combat it. After all, government funding already exists for free food and free housing for the poor and even free money for the unemployed, but the parameters are misunderstood and the results are weak at best. A full revamping of this system is needed.

> *We need to look at the psychology behind homelessness and poverty and understand how to combat it.*

Rather than throwing money at different problems and hoping they go away, we should take an active role in helping to get people back on their feet as contributing members of society. It shouldn't be segmented; you are either making it or you are not. There has always been an unspoken tier of support; first the family attempts to help, then the community, then the government. The last resort option is too often a first choice for people who seek to take advantage of the system.

> *Rather than throwing money at different problems and hoping they go away, we should take an active role in helping to get people back on their feet as contributing members of society.*

Only once a person is completely at the end of all potential help and opportunity should they turn to the government. First and foremost, this should not be treated as a shameful thing. When a person shows up at a hospital with cancer, they are not shamed for it but brought in and comforted. What would be shameful would be to hide it and let it fester until it kills you. But for whatever reason, we view mental and social issues as the opposite. We shame people for bringing them to light and have an unspoken respect for people who bottle up their problems. People who come forward with problems should not be defined by them, but rather applauded for their courage and given the tools needed to overcome them.

> **People who come forward with problems should not be defined by them, but rather applauded for their courage and given the tools needed to overcome them.**

The government recovery program needs to be relatively strict. An ideal set up would be a sort of financial and psychological halfway house. Each house would have a certain number of government employed mentors who would act as the supervisors, counselors, and career advisors all at once. Everyone would be required to continue to educate themselves while they are in the program, as well as working towards employment, or risk going back out on the street. We have to be very careful when striking the balance between helping people and enabling bad behaviors. This type of system, and really any type of recovery system, can only be effective on people who want to be helped. This

> **We have to be very careful when striking the balance between helping people and enabling bad behaviors.**

program could also be easily funded by the combined budgets of food stamps, government housing, unemployment, and the millions of empty homes for use across the country.

The newly implemented system would not only benefit just the textbook homeless person either. In a constantly growing and changing economy, there will continue to be positions and even entire industries that are created and destroyed. One quickly approaching industry is the taxi industry; once self-driving cars are fully implemented then we will have an entire industry of unemployed taxi drivers. Where are they to go, and what are they to do? We need to make sure that our country is set up to protect those who are willing to participate and not cut anyone out for their contribution, whether it is now a piece of history or soon to be a piece of the future.

Last but not least, the whole notion of The Never Ending Brainstorm is to continue to advance as a society. We need to constantly be looking to see what our goals are as a society, and taking realistic steps together to achieve those. Much like the absorption of the financial industry, there are other facets of our country that should be brought under the public domain, using Maslow's Hierarchy as a guide. Things

> *We need to constantly be looking to see what our goals are as a society, and taking realistic steps together to achieve those.*

like electricity, plumbing, and running water are things that every person will use every day, and most of the time we don't even have a choice as to our provider. If every commercial electric company and water treatment and utility company were to be brought under the Department of Utilities and fees made to be a tax, a change like that would simplify the lives of every person in this country.

Every building you ever entered would always have power and running water, and bills would never have to be switched. Even internet, phone, and cell phone service could fall under the same model. All hardware could remain under the bubble of capitalism, but the service itself would fall under a department of the government. Again, it is of the utmost importance that none of these changes take place without power being brought back into the hands

> *It is of the utmost importance that none of these changes take place without power being brought back into the hands of the people.*

94

of the people. Further centralization of the government while it is still fully controlled by the financial oligarchy would only mean further disaster for the American people.

The point is, the potential for our society is unlimited. When we put our heads together and think like rational people, rather than fighting over trivial issues that don't impact our lives 99% of the time, then we can achieve great things. What is the final goal, after all? In a world where everything is at our fingertips and everyone has everything they need, then the main goal is efficiency. How can we get food, water, and shelter to every person as easily as possible, so everyone can focus on innovating and creating new great things? The more money you can spend on your friends' and neighbors' cool ideas, the more they will have to spend on yours. Once we can get both money and resources flowing smoothly and effectively, only then can The Never Ending Brainstorm truly achieve its full potential.

CLOSING THOUGHTS

The Never Ending Brainstorm is not a static concept. It is a living, breathing, fluid mentality that encompasses the collective thoughts of humanity. If no one person has all the answers, then each and every one of us should constantly strive towards understanding other perspectives and deciding for ourselves what is best. Logic and science need to be at the core of all beliefs and ideas, and as a society we need to learn how to disagree with each other more effectively. This starts with the individual, then moves to the education system, and finally into the world of policy.

If we cannot figure out how to appropriately interact one on one, how much more so will those problems be exacerbated at the state and national levels! The culture of political correctness and being offended is reaching a point of absurdity. Sure, there are some people who specifically say and do things with the purpose of being offensive. John Stuart Mill said it best in his writing, "On Liberty of Thought and Discussion." He asserted that, "the peculiar evil of silencing the expression of an opinion is, that it is robbing the human race... If the opinion is right, they are deprived of the opportunity of exchanging error for truth: if wrong, they lose, what is almost as great a benefit, the clearer perception and livelier impression of truth, produced by its collision with error" (Mill). It is our job to treat people's opinions with respect and also to think critically about them. After all, that is what most people expect others to do.

If the public can reach a consensus that this is the most logical and most promising course of action, then immediate changes to education need to take place. Steps need to be made to become more like the successful education systems of the world, such as utilizing interteaching, relaxing the environment for students, and giving teachers more respect and power over their curriculum. Logic and science need to be a regular focus, and should be re-emphasized every year along with every other subject that is taught. Finally, students need to understand real world practicability, and work towards becoming a member of society that is needed, matched with their abilities and interests. Only once the general public understands these things can any real political or economic change take place.

This is where the most crucial steps are. The laws in our country are overly complex, and the allowance for corruption is reaching a boiling point. All of the resources we need are right in front of us to create a society that is well informed and participates regularly in political processes. Greater understanding of the strengths and weaknesses of individualism and collectivism will allow us more flexibility in what we centralize and what we leave to the free market. Most importantly, a society of people that believe in the concepts of The Never Ending Brainstorm will result in balanced and respectful political discussions. This will maximize personal freedoms and the efficiency of protective measures that need to be taken.

When all of these steps are taken, true societal evolution can begin to take place. And not just societal evolution, but intentional societal evolution. There are so many things that we are capable of, both as individuals and as a whole. All too often, that potential is wasted due to a lack of understanding and a lack of effort. The more we begin to understand each other and intentionally work towards creating a better society together, the more quickly our dreams can come to fruition. Only by changing the way that we disagree with each other can we create true intentional societal evolution.

EPILOGUE

Logic Based Faith

I have included my own religious belief as a part of this document in what I believe is a logic based faith. I do not do this with intent to change minds, although that is not something I am opposed to either. Instead, I include it just so you can see another perspective on philosophy and on what exists beyond our physical universe. I believe I have made it overwhelmingly clear that I am open to hearing any point of view, I sincerely hope that if you disagree with my religious beliefs that you do not allow it to sway your opinion of everything else up to this point.

Personally, I make every effort to have my beliefs grounded in logic. I was raised in a strict evangelical Christian family. I was fortunate enough to have parents who taught me to question everything including my own faith, which is a concept also found in the Bible. I knew that if God had given humans logic, he did so that we may discern for ourselves what is right and wrong, along with any guidelines that we have from history. When the time came for me to attend college, I made a conscious effort to learn about every other religion. If I was going to be a Christian, it was going to be because I believed it and not because my parents told me to. After studying world religions collegiately, I dove in to many original religious texts and truly broke down their beliefs.

What I found was that logically, I felt two religions really make the most sense. Of course, all of this mental deliberation is done utilizing a set of assumptions. The first assumption, of course, is that a higher power exists of some kind. The second assumption follows the laws of energy conservation, in that the consciousness/soul of every human lives on after death. Almost every religion in the world relies upon these two assumptions, although many run into some logical problems along the way.

The majority of religions have the concept of a good and a bad afterlife, with different means of qualifying to get in. The good afterlife usually entails getting to live in commune with the creator/spirit/deity that is worshipped in that particular religion. Most also ascertain that the deity is perfect: omniscient, omnipotent, and omnipresent. Unfortunately, what this means is that to be able to live alongside the perfect being, one must become perfect as well. A good analogy of this concept is a laundry basket. If you put two clean white shirts in, they can both stay clean. But if one of the shirts is dirty at all it will taint the perfection of the other shirt. It doesn't matter if the second shirt is covered in mud or just has a speck of dust on it, it is enough to taint the perfection of the other.

You would be hard pressed to find a person that would be willing to say they have never done anything wrong, much less a person who actually means it or believes it. Everyone on earth has done at least one thing wrong in their lives, it is human nature! This is where I believe many religious beliefs miss the mark. Most religions try to make the follower the hero of the story. Whether it is by trying to do more good deeds than bad and keeping the scale over 51%, or if it is performing sacrifices and rituals for every deed done wrong, all action-based options will always fall short because it is impossible as just a human to achieve the mark of perfection.

This is where Christianity distinguishes itself. Unlike all other religions, salvation has nothing to do with a set of actions or a scale of any kind. Rather, it requires accepting that nothing we do is good enough, and that our own sinful actions are more than enough reason to exclude us from paradise. Christianity holds that Jesus was the only perfect human, empowered as the Son of God, and was the only human ever deserving of entering heaven on his own accord.

But instead, he chose to die for all the sins of humanity and endure three days of punishment so we would not have to, like when a classmate in school offers to take a punishment so another student does not have to bear the pain that they rightfully should.

The only role of the Christian in all of this is to acknowledge what Jesus did, accept the gift of his sacrifice, and strive to live life better. There is no magical switch that makes people better, but rather that the love of God and surrounding yourself with positive influences can help you to become a better person. Too many Christians get caught up arguing in some of the details of potentially less relevant scripture, or try to argue against science such as macro evolution in thinking that it goes against the Bible. If anything, from a creationist perspective the concept of evolution makes God seem even more powerful than the Bible does!

Again, in keeping with the concepts of logic and science, we have to be open to the possibility that macro evolution is real, but also open to the possibility that it is not. It is important to remember though, that if Christians believe that all humans are flawed, and if we understand that the Bible was scribed by humans and translated by humans, then we have to understand that there may be some imperfections in what we are reading. Fortunately, that is why God also blessed each of us with a conscience and the ability to use logic, so that we may decipher the truth from it.

Jesus understood this as well, which is why part of what he came back to do was to change the way the law had been corrupted. Too many Christians also read the Bible out of context; and it is important to understand which parts are history, which parts are parables, and which parts are actually commandments and rules for religious living. In the Bible, Jesus actually broke multiple Old Testament laws, so if you truly believe that those are sins then that invalidates the entirety of the Christian theology. Fortunately, Jesus told us what is important. When the Pharisees confronted him over one of the rules he broke, he corrected them and said all that mattered were two things: loving God with everything you have and loving your neighbor as yourself. If you can do those two things, everything else falls into place.

The final area where many Christians slip up is in judging other people. The Bible makes it very clear that God is the only one who can truly judge. On one hand, Jesus said that he is the way, the truth, and the life, and that no one comes to the father except through him. On the other hand, he also said to seek the kingdom of God and you will find it. It does not say that you need to come to the conclusion that Christianity is the correct choice and you will find heaven, but simply that if you are seeking it you will find it. It is possible that this is more inclusive than many Christians believe it is.

Pretend for a moment that Christianity is right, and it is the Christian God in heaven. All of the Muslim people out there, kneeling down every day to pray to Allah to help them to be a better person and to seek the truth, there's no way God hears those prayers and goes "Allah? Who's this Allah guy?" and ignores them. The same would be true in reverse; if it is Allah that is up there then there is no way he ignores the prayers to Jesus either. The point is, from a practical standpoint it is not the place of the person to judge, but only God. Our job is to live life with kindness and spread our message wherever it is readily accepted.

As I mentioned before; I believe there to be two logically possible religions, and the second of these is the concept of Karma/reincarnation in Buddhism and Hinduism. Without breaking any of the assumptions listed above (the existence of a higher power and the immortality of the human soul), then Karma could logically work as well. With an infinite number of reincarnation attempts, it is hypothetically possible that one could achieve perfection over a set of lifetimes, allowing the newly perfected soul to transcend this universe for the next one. Perhaps, even, our own Jesus was one of these very few people to achieve this level of perfection.

The reason that I choose to believe Christianity over Karma is simple. The first is that if Jesus was as I just described, then the message he delivered would be inconsistent with that reality. The second reason is the most important; in that by living a life aligned with Christ one meets all of the requirements of Karma, but the reverse is not true. Just as with any of my other opinions, if I am to encounter proof or a reason to believe contrary to my current belief system, then I will adopt that into my worldview and adjust accordingly. But, for the time being, my set of principles and beliefs are founded in logic and simplicity, and I plan to keep them that way.

SOURCES REFERENCED

Britannica Editors. "Laws of Thought." Encyclopædia

Britannica, Inc., 14 Sept. 2016.

https://www.britannica.com/topic/laws-of-thought

Bronson, Richard. "Homeless and Empty Homes -- an

American Travesty." Huffington Post. 24 Aug. 2010.

http://www.huffingtonpost.com/richard-skip-

bronson/post_733_b_692546.html

Bryant, Elizabeth. "France Battles Food Waste by Law."

DW.COM. Deutsche Welle, 19 Apr. 2016.

http://www.dw.com/en/france-battles-food-waste-

by-law/a-19148931

D'Orio, Wayne. "Finland Is #1!" Finland Is #1! Scholastic.

http://www.scholastic.com/browse/article.jsp?id=37

49880

Kolbert, Elizabeth. "Why Facts Don't Change Our Minds."

The New Yorker, 17 Feb. 2017.

http://www.newyorker.com/magazine/2017/02/27/

why-facts-dont-change-our-minds

Kurtzleben, Danielle. "Canada Reminds Us That American

Elections Are Much Longer." NPR., 21 Oct. 2015.

http://www.npr.org/sections/itsallpolitics/2015/10/

21/450238156/canadas-11-week-campaign-

reminds-us-that-american-elections-are-much-

longer

Mass, Warren. "Princeton/Northwestern Study Seems to

Conclude U.S. an Oligarchy." The New American.

Princeton University, 24 Apr. 2014.

http://www.thenewamerican.com/usnews/constitut

ion/item/18120-princeton-northwestern-study-

seems-to-conclude-u-s-an-oligarchy

McCaig, Amy. "First Worldwide Survey of Religion and

Science." Rice University, 3 Dec. 2015.

http://news.rice.edu/2015/12/03/first-worldwide-

survey-of-religion-and-science-no-not-all-scientists-

are-atheists/

Mill, John Stuart. "Of the Liberty of Thought and

Discussion." On Liberty. London: Longmans, Green,

1882. Print.

Saville, Bryan K. "Interteaching: Ten Tips for Effective

Implementation." APS. Association for Psychological

Science, 31 Jan. 2013.

http://www.psychologicalscience.org/observer/inter

teaching-ten-tips-for-effective-

implementation#.WJE9SVMrKUk

Scutti, Susan. "Do Video Games Lead to Violence?" CNN.

Cable News Network, 26 July 2016.

http://www.cnn.com/2016/07/25/health/video-

games-and-violence/

Stone, Chad. "A Guide to Statistics on Historical Trends in

Income Inequality." CBPP.org. Center on Budget and

Policy Priorities, 7 Nov. 2016.

http://www.cbpp.org/research/poverty-and-

inequality/a-guide-to-statistics-on-historical-trends-

in-income-inequality

ABOUT THE AUTHOR

Tyler James Rits was born in Austin, Texas, in 1991 to an Air Force family. He moved all over the world, eventually going to UCF for college and settling down in Jupiter, Florida with his wife Chloe. He first became interested in social change while living in DC during the events of 2001. From then on, it was his life's goal to solve major social and political issues. He began studying, worked at a state capitol, pursued his interests at a collegiate level, and has continued to reform his ideas through logical discourse with friends and family. He received a Bachelor's in Political Science and a Bachelor's in Psychology from the University of Central Florida in 2013, and has worked in both business and mental health counseling since then. His goal is to improve our society through rational discussion, and is available to anyone who has thoughts or questions about his ideas!